PREDATORS!

PREDATORS

BY ANITA BASKIN-SALZBERG AND
ALLEN SALZBERG

FRANKLIN WATTS
NEW YORK LONDON TORONTO SYDNEY
A FIRST BOOK 1991

Cover photograph of a giant grizzly bear comes courtesy of
Tom Edwards/Wildlife Photographer
Title page: A western gull enjoys a starfish dinner.
Photographs courtesy of: Jeff Foott: pp. 2, 8, 14; DRK Photo: pp. 10, 39, 49, 53 (all
Stephen J. Krasemann), 18 (Jeff Foott), 30 top (Don & Pat Valenti), 30 bottom (Jett
Britnell), 32 (S. Nielsen), 40 bottom (Michael Fogden), 44 (M.P. Kahl), 46 bottom (John
Gerlach); Animals Animals: pp. 12 (Breck P. Kent), 21, 56 (both Zig Leszczynski), 26
(Fritz Prenzel), 34 (G.I. Bernard), 35 (OSF/Steven Dalton), 46 top (Arthur Gloor), 48
(Anup & Manoj Shah); Paul E. Meyers: p. 40 top.

Library of Congress Cataloging-in-Publication Data

Baskin-Salzberg, Anita.
Predators! / by Anita Baskin-Salzberg and Allen Salzberg.
p.   cm. — (A First book)
Includes bibliographical references and index.
Summary: Discusses the feeding habits and hunting methods of
various predatory animals, demonstrating how they maintain the food
chain.
ISBN 0-531-20009-4
1. Predatory animals—Juvenile literature.   2. Predation
(Biology)—Juvenile literature.   [1. Predatory animals.]
I. Salzberg, Allen.   II. Title.   III. Series.
QL758.B37   1991
591.53—dc20   90-47672 CIP AC

CONTENTS

To my sister, Ann,
who always believed.
—A. S.

And to our parents,
who were always there for us.
—A. B. S. and A. S.

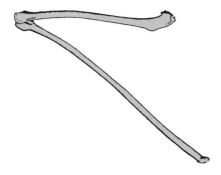

A killer whale ventures dangerously near the shoreline to grab a sea lion meal.

1
A PREDATOR'S PLACE
IN THE WORLD

A group of penguins sun themselves on an ice floe. Splash! Hunger drives them into the cold water to hunt for fish. Soon the hunter becomes the hunted as a penguin finds itself in the jaws of a leopard seal, who kills it with a quick crunch. Its stomach full of penguin, the seal now climbs onto the empty ice to rest.

Suddenly, the hunter again becomes the hunted as the ice floe is surrounded by a pack of orcas, or killer whales. The doomed seal clings to the ice. It's only a matter of time until the intelligent orcas figure out a way to move the seal off the ice and into their waiting jaws.

Does this story make you feel upset or sad? Did you think that the seals or the orcas were downright evil?

That's not unusual. When it comes to *predators*, or animals that catch, kill, and eat other animals called *prey*, many people have strong emotions. To us, killing other an-

This picture of a hyena stealing part of another animal's kill may shock you. But would you be as disturbed by a picture of a person eating a chicken leg?

imals may seem cruel. But predators have no choice. They must kill to survive.

TYPES OF PREDATORS

Predators come in all shapes and sizes and live all over the world, from the cold Arctic to the hot African desert. A tiny ladybug that feeds on small insects is just as much a predator as a 1,000-pound (454 kg) grizzly bear that feasts on fish, deer, or ground squirrels. Even a pet cat that catches birds in the backyard is a predator.

People are predators too. When we sit down to a dinner of chicken, hamburger, or fish, we are eating another animal. We are different from most predators because someone else has killed that animal for us.

Some predators including cats, crocodiles, hawks, snakes, frogs, dragonflies, and spiders eat only other animals. They are called *carnivores,* or *strict predators.*

Predators that eat plants, leaves, nuts, and berries as well as meat are called *omnivores,* or *part-time predators.*

As you've seen, a predator can itself become prey for a larger or stronger predator. In fact, only the biggest, fastest, most powerful predators don't become a meal for another animal. They are called *apex,* or *top predators.* Top predators include wolves, orcas, tigers, and birds of prey. Figure 1 gives examples of top predators and their prey.

Most top predators are carnivores. But the grizzly bear is one example of a top predator that is an omnivore.

What kind of predator do you think we are? Like the grizzly bear, humans are top predators and omnivores.

*Raccoons have been called "little people,"
because of their humanlike hands and taste for
almost everything people eat, including apples.*

FIGURE 1.
WHO EATS WHOM?
TOP PREDATORS OF THE WORLD

PREDATOR/HABITAT	PHYSICAL CHARACTERISTICS	PREY
Killer Whale, or Orca—every ocean of the world	Can grow to 30 feet (9.1 m) long and weigh 9 tons (8.163 metric tons)	Seals, sea lions, dolphins, porpoises, salmon, minke and grey whales, fish, and sometimes birds
Lion—Africa and India	Males: 9 to 10 feet (2.7 to 3 m) long and up to 500 pounds (227 kg) Females: 7 to 8 feet (2.1 to 2.4 m) long and up to 300 pounds (136 kg)	Wildebeest, water buffalo, antelope, zebra, gnu, Thompson's gazelle
Grizzly Bear—Northwest Canada, Alaska, the western United States, and the Soviet Union	Can weigh between 400 and 850 pounds (181 and 385 kg) and grow to 7 feet (2.1 m) long	Salmon, ground squirrels, lemmings, mice, insects, small rodents
Polar Bear—the Arctic Circle (Soviet Union, Norway, Greenland, Canada and the United States)	Can weigh between 900 and 1,000 pounds (408 and 454 kg) and grow to 8 feet (2.4 m) long	Seals, salmon, lemmings, waterfowl, walrus
Bald Eagle—North America	White head and tail, massive yellow beak and feet, 10 to 12 pounds (4.5 to 5.4 kg)	Fish, waterfowl, rabbits, and squirrels
Saltwater Crocodile—From eastern India to the Philippines and North Australia	Can grow to be 21 feet (6.4 m) long and weigh one ton (.9 metric t)	Turtles, snakes, rats, insects, snails, and small fish
Tiger—India, Turkey, the Soviet Union, China, parts of Southeast Asia	A male Siberian tiger weighs more than 600 pounds (272 kg) and can measure 10 feet (3 m) long	Wild boar, deer, moose, Indian buffalo

The giant grizzly bear, like the raccoon, is a part-time predator.

THE FOOD CHAIN

Predators play an important role in nature. All predators are part of a food chain. Scientists use the term food chain to describe the way in which energy is passed from one organism to another.

Figure 2 shows how a typical food chain works. Plants are the first link in most food chains. Through *photosynthesis*, they use the sun's energy to make food. Then animals such as caterpillars and sheep eat the plants. Predators such as birds and foxes in turn eat the plant eaters. They may, in turn, become a meal for a top predator. Each time one animal eats another, a small bit of the sun's energy is passed along the chain.

When plants and animals die, bacteria and fungi in the soil break their bodies down into their chemical components. This decomposed matter adds important nutrients to the soil that help new plants transform the sun's energy into food. And so it begins a new food chain.

Most natural communities have several food chains that interconnect. Two or more connecting food chains are called a food web. An animal can be part of more than one food chain. For instance, a mouse can be part of a food chain with a top predator like a great horned owl. Or it can be part of a food chain with a smaller predator like a fox.

A food pyramid is a diagram that shows how much food an animal must eat to survive. Figure 3 shows a food pyramid that can be found in Pelham Bay Park in the Bronx. This park is just 10 miles (16 km) from downtown New York City.

As you can see, it takes a lot of grass to support a population of field mice. And it takes a lot of field mice to

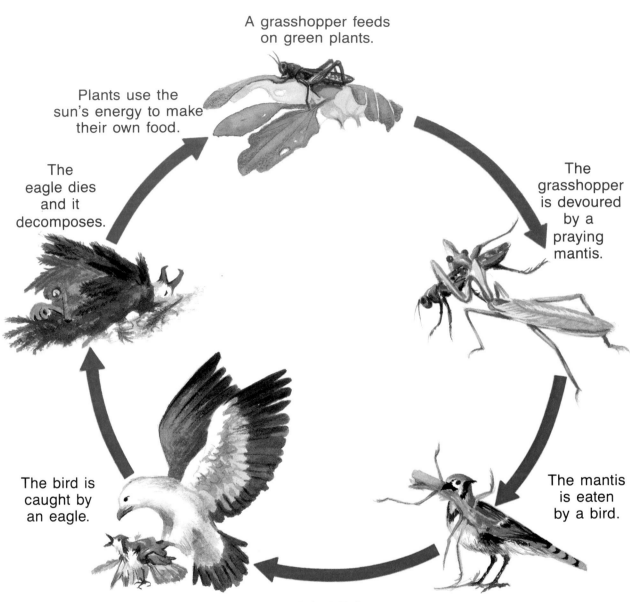

A grasshopper feeds on green plants.

Plants use the sun's energy to make their own food.

The eagle dies and it decomposes.

The grasshopper is devoured by a praying mantis.

The bird is caught by an eagle.

The mantis is eaten by a bird.

FIGURE 2.
A FOOD CHAIN

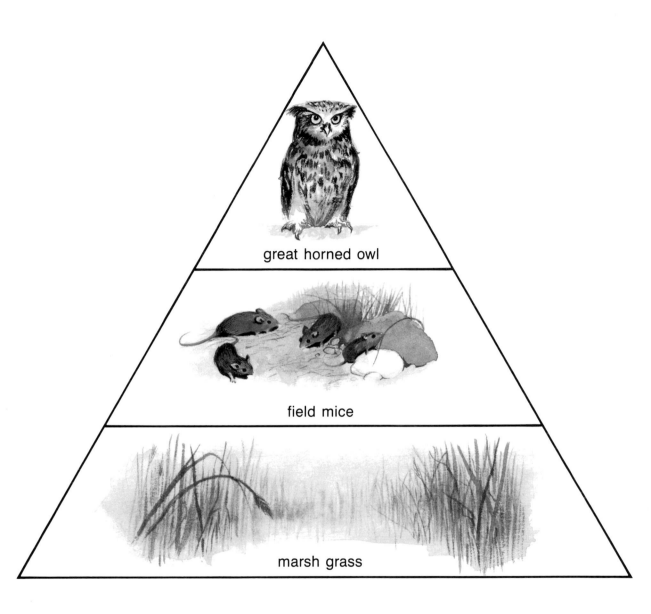

FIGURE 3.
A FOOD PYRAMID

feed one great horned owl, which can eat its own weight in mice in one night!

A food pyramid shows why there are always many more plant eaters than predators and more small predators than apex predators. If this weren't so, predators would eat all of the prey animals and starve to death.

But what if the grass in the pyramid was sprayed with a *pesticide?* The pesticide will remain in the body of any animal that eats the grass. So when the owl eats hundreds of grass-eating mice, the amount of poison in the owl's body will total all of the poison in all of the mice it has eaten.

When pesticides like DDT are absorbed by eagles and other birds of prey, it causes them to lay eggs with thin shells that crack before any babies can hatch.

If the pesticide in the pyramid had killed the mice outright, predators like the owl that rely on a diet of mice would starve. When people harm the environment, top predators are soon affected.

Because pesticides like DDT used to build up in fish tissue, fish-eating bald eagles were once threatened with extinction.

2
FINDING FOOD—THE BETTER TO SEE YOU WITH

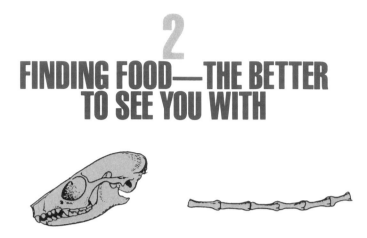

On a calm, dark night, a great horned owl sits high up in a tree and listens alertly. Suddenly, its ears pick up the faint scamperings of a field mouse. Silently, the owl launches itself from its perch and flies directly toward the sound, guided only by its hearing. Still too far away to see its prey, the owl uses its large eyes to navigate through a maze of trees and bushes. Seconds later, it has seized and killed the mouse with its sharp claws.

The owl's superb hearing and vision are considered to be among the best in the animal kingdom. These remarkable senses, along with the strong claws and soft feathers that allow the owl to fly without making a sound, help it to find and catch its dinner.

In fact, all predators have one or two remarkably well-developed senses to help them locate prey. There are even predators with unusual senses, such as bats who "see" with their own kind of *sonar*.

Most owls eat rats, mice, shrews, squirrels, birds, snakes, lizards, and spiders. A long-eared owl will eat all of these animals, but it prefers rodents.

SEEING

Vision is often a predator's most important sense. Many predators rely on vision for the final capture of prey, even if they've scented it or heard it first.

A predator's eyes are usually located in the front of its head, as are those of humans. This gives it some degree of binocular, or three-dimensional, vision. That is, the area that each eye sees overlaps, so the brain receives two slightly different messages about the same scene. These differences enable a predator to tell how far away a prey animal is and how fast it is running or flying.

Most prey animals' eyes are on either side of their heads. This position gives these animals a wide field of view so they can see what predators are sneaking up from behind!

Superb vision helps insects and birds to fly, land, and catch prey in midair. A bird of prey's telescope-like vision can be eight times better than ours is. It is so good, in fact, that an eagle flying high in the air can easily spy a grasshopper in a meadow hundreds of feet below.

Each of our eyes has a single lens that sees only one image at a time. But the *compound eyes* of insects contain thousands of lenses that allow them to see thousands of images at the same time. With the largest compound eyes in the insect world, a dragonfly, for example, can spot prey from almost any angle.

There are even predators with more than two eyes! Spiders and scorpions have clusters of six to eight eyes. The jumping spider's four large main eyes form the image. Its smaller front eyes estimate distance, and the two remaining eyes on the side of its head detect motion. However, even with eight eyes, a spider can only see about 1 foot (0.3 m) in front of its face!

On a bright moonlit night, the amount of light with which to see is millions of times less than during the day. That's why nocturnal predators, or animals that hunt at night, like cats, bears, and alligators, have a special mirror-like structure in the back of their eyes. This structure is called a tapetum, and it helps these animals to see in the dark. Sharks, whales, and fish that hunt in the dark ocean also have a tapetum in their eyes.

The tapetum allows cats to see with about one-sixth as much light as we need and owls to see with 100 times less light than humans. In fact, an owl sees as well in near-total darkness as you or I see in broad daylight.

HEARING

For locating food, hearing a meal running through the grass can be just as important to a predator as seeing it run, especially when the light is dim. Animals like coyotes and lions move their ears forward and back like antennae in order to pinpoint the direction of a sound.

Some animals don't need ears to hear! Instead, these animals discover where a meal is by feeling vibrations in their bodies. Ground vibrations from moving prey animals are transmitted through the bones of salamanders and snakes to nerves near their ears.

Sharks, and many other fish, monitor vibrations in the water with their *lateral-line system*. This system consists of fluid-filled canals that lie just beneath the shark's skin along the sides of its head and body. The canals are filled with small pores open to the water. Underwater noise or motion causes a vibration that strikes these open pores and sends a message to the shark's brain that a meal may be within reach.

SMELLING

Just as you smell food cooking in the kitchen, some predators can also smell a meal—but from almost a mile (1.6 km) away.

Although a fox's hearing is superb, its sense of smell is even better. A fox can smell a dead animal, even when it's under 2 feet (0.61 m) of soil. Wolves and coyotes can track the scent an animal has left with its paws.

In murky water, a good nose is more useful than a pair of sharp eyes. A shark can smell so well that some scientists call it a "swimming nose." The shark's nostrils—which have nothing to do with breathing—are filled with olfactory cells, the cells that sense odors. Water constantly flows in and out of each nostril, bathing these cells with odor-laden water. As a result, some species of sharks can smell prey from over 2 miles (3.2 km) away.

Snakes smell with their tongues! When a snake flicks its tongue in and out of its mouth, it's not getting ready to bite. It's smelling the air by picking up particles of dust, which the snake's tongue carries into taste detectors in the mouth called the Jacobson's Organ. The taste of these particles tells the snake what animals are near. When a poisonous snake bites prey that escapes and later dies, its

Jacobson's Organ enables the snake to find the dead animal, even when that animal is out of sight.

SUPER SENSES

Some predators are not limited to our five senses of sight, sound, smell, taste, and touch. Sharks and other fish can locate their dinner by detecting the electrical field given off by their prey's nervous system. Weak-sighted or blind deep-water fish find prey by setting up their own electrical field that works like an electrical spider web. The moment an unwary fish disturbs the field, the predator grabs its meal.

Fighter pilots and submarine navigators locate enemy planes and ships with radar and sonar. These are radio and sound signals transmitted through the air or water that bounce off the enemy and back to the pilot. Toothed dolphins, porpoises, and many species of bats locate food with their own type of sonar called *echolocation.* That is, they send out streams of *ultrasonic* "clicks" too high-pitched for humans to hear. These clicks are focused into a narrow beam of sound that the animal sweeps back and forth as you would a flashlight.

Each click is just a millisecond long. It echoes off a fish or insect and back to the predator, who "reads" the returning echoes to get a picture of the size and shape of its prey and the predator's distance from it. Echolocation cannot only tell a horseshoe bat exactly where a juicy insect is located, but which way the insect is flying.

Some boa constrictors, pythons, and snakes called pit vipers, which include rattlesnakes and copperheads, use a

special kind of vision to find prey in total darkness. They form a heat-sensitive image of their prey with the cone-shaped holes, or "pits," under each eye. There are at least 150,000 heat-sensitive nerve cells in each pit. These cells register the heat (actually an invisible kind of light called *infrared* light) given off by warm-blooded animals.

Mites and mosquitoes also respond to infrared light. To find a warm-blooded victim, a female mosquito uses heat-sensitive antennae less than ⅛ of an inch (.61 cm) long. Keep that in mind the next time you're bitten by an insect on a hot, muggy day.

The pit viper hunts by sensing changes in temperature as it lies in wait or crawls along slowly, moving its head from side to side. Even the difference of a thousandth of a degree Fahrenheit alerts the snake to a warm-blooded creature passing within striking distance.

3
WEAPONS—OUCH!

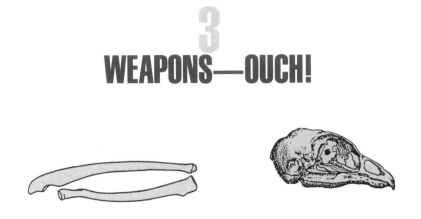

Imagine that in order to eat, you have to kill your dinner with your hands, your teeth, or your nails! That's exactly what predators must do. That is, they use parts of their bodies as weapons to kill their prey. Some snakes called constrictors even use their entire body as a weapon. They wrap themselves around their prey and squeeze hard until the animal stops breathing.

Because of a predator's arsenal of weapons, a predator's size has nothing to do with how deadly it is. With its strong legs and jaws, a praying mantis is just as dangerous to its insect prey as a tiger is to a 200-pound (90.7 kg) deer.

The main weapons of the animal world are sharp teeth and claws and powerful jaws. Not only do teeth and claws help most predators to kill their prey, they also act as a predator's knife and fork, helping it to hold and cut its food.

TEETH

Most animals have three kinds of teeth. The sharp front incisors cut food. Longer, dangerous-looking pointed teeth on each side of the mouth called canines tear off big hunks of flesh. Flat, strong molars at the back of the mouth chew or grind plants.

Carnivores like wolves and big cats may hold struggling prey with their front incisors. They then kill by sinking their sharp canines deep into the necks or throats of their victims.

Even with strong, sharp teeth, predators like sharks and crocodiles must swallow their food in large chunks. Instead of using their teeth for biting or chewing, these predators use their long, cone-shaped teeth for grasping and pulling large animals under water until they drown.

Most fish have teeth, but few can chew. Instead, rows of pointed, pin-sharp teeth spear and hold tight to slippery dinners. Fish must also swallow their meals whole or tear off large chunks to down in big gulps.

BEAKS AND CLAWS

Not every predator has teeth. Birds of prey, or *raptors*, have powerful hooked beaks made of horn that work just as well as teeth. Raptors use their strong beaks to break the spine of a prey animal or to tear the animal apart.

Other birds' beaks, or bills, are adapted to the prey they capture. These birds may even use their bills as tools that drill, hammer, or chisel. Bee eaters reach way down into

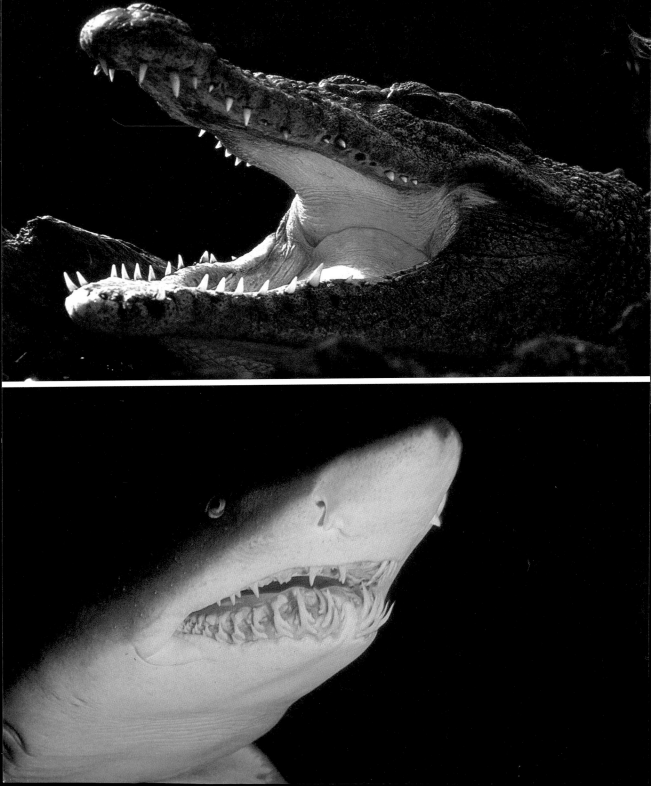

flowers for juicy insects with their long, narrow bills. King-fishers spear fish with their long, pointed beaks. Woodpeckers bore into the barks of trees for grubs and insects with their hard bills.

Sharp claws are also powerful weapons. The long curved claws of raptors are called talons. The hawk's wide-spreading talons get a good grip on squirming birds that the hawk catches on the fly. Ospreys and bald eagles fish by hovering over the water, then dropping down feet first to snag a fish with its talons on each foot.

Except for the cheetah, all big cats have formidable claws that they use to grip and tear. Cats pull in their claws when they run to keep them sharp. Moles and hedgehogs burrow for insects with their claws, while grizzly bears dig up roots and burrowing rodents with theirs. Claws can also be just

(Top) Few animals escape from a crocodile's jaws, which may have as much as half a ton of gripping power! (Bottom) Everyone knows that sharks have huge, frightening teeth. But did you know that most sharks have five sets of teeth? As the shark's front teeth wear out, they're quickly replaced by the set behind. Many species of sharks are born with a mouth full of teeth, ready to feed on any smaller animal.

The great blue heron's long
beak makes a good spear.

the tip of the weapon. Grizzly bears are so strong that they can kill with one blow from a powerful paw.

TONGUES

For some predators, a tongue is a very effective weapon. Nature's fastest tongue belongs to the slow-moving chameleon. The chameleon captures and swallows unlucky insect victims in a split second by "firing" its long sticky tongue at them. The giant anteater captures food with a tongue as long as a person's arm.

POISON

Nature has given predators a number of other powerful hunting weapons, including poison. Examples of the most dangerous poisonous predators are given in Figure 4.

Snakes inject their poison through the channels in their deadly *fangs.* The poison paralyzes or kills their prey so the snake can swallow it whole. The jaws of most snakes can be unhinged from each other so that the snake's mouth can open very wide. A snake can easily swallow a meal that is much bigger than its own head!

Unlike snakes, spiders can't swallow prey whole. Instead, after injecting its poison, the spider releases strong digestive enzymes that turn the prey's insides to liquid. Then the spider sucks up this "soup" with its strawlike mouth.

The use of fangs is only one way to inject poison. Wasps and scorpions paralyze and kill their meals with powerful poison *stingers,* while jellyfish kill theirs with deadly poison *tentacles.*

The archer fish's aim is very accurate. It almost never misses a shot. It curls its tongue against the roof of its mouth to form a tube that shoots bullets of water several feet up in the air.

These bullets knock insects off twigs and branches and into the water, where the fish quickly swallows them.

The end of a chameleon's tongue is coated with a gluelike substance that prey will stick to.

FIGURE 4.
THE DEADLIEST POISONOUS PREDATORS

SPECIES	TERRITORY	PREY
Geographic Cone Snail	Australia and South Pacific Islands	Fish
Blue-ringed Octopus	Australia	Fish, crabs, and other small marine animals
Sea Wasp Jellyfish	Australia	Small fish
Scorpions	Tropical and subtropical areas like Africa and Egypt	Small insects and invertebrates
Black Widow Spider	United States	Small insects
Sydney Funnel-Web Spider	Australia	Small insects
Green Mamba Snake	Southeast and central Africa	Small mammals, birds, occasional lizard or frog
Taipan Snake	Northeast Australia and New Guinea	Rats and mice

ELECTRICITY

Electric rays and eels have another weapon that helps them capture a good meal—electricity. Rays rest on the ocean bottom, waiting for a fish to swim by. When it does, a jolt of electricity stuns or kills it. Freshwater electric eels can deliver a punch of 1,000 volts—enough power to kill a horse!

Scientists believe that dolphins, orcas, and beluga and sperm whales can produce a powerful sound beam from within their heads with which they actually stun their prey!

4
CAMOUFLAGE—A DANGEROUS GAME OF HIDE-AND-SEEK

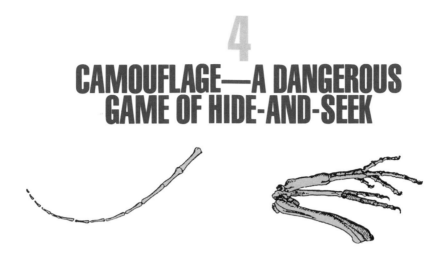

A praying mantis stands perfectly still on a branch. After a few hours, a choice insect wanders within reach of the mantis's strong, deadly legs. Even if the insect were to look right at the mantis, it probably would not see it. That's because the mantis's green coat blends perfectly with the green branch it sits on. Since the branch camouflages, or disguises, the mantis, the insect sees the branch but not the mantis.

Camouflage is nature's clever way of protecting both predators and prey. An animal's natural camouflage, that is, the color of its coat or the shape of its body, helps it to merge with its background.

Camouflage helps predators sneak up on their victims undetected. Surprise can mean the difference between a good meal and an empty stomach. For prey animals, protective camouflage can spell life or death.

NATURAL CAMOUFLAGE

There are three basic kinds of natural camouflage. The first is *color resemblance*, in which an animal's color resembles, or looks like, that of its natural surroundings, as the mantis's does. A lion's tawny coat, which matches the sandy plains of its African home, is another good example. So is the leopard's yellow-and-black coat that conceals the animal in the dappled forest. Color resemblance explains why desert animals are usually tan and jungle animals are green.

This type of camouflage helps predators stalk and ambush prey while the predator is in full view! It can also save a predator from becoming a victim itself. A bright red crab spider sitting on a red flower is almost impossible for a bee (the spider's favorite food) to spot until it's too late. Luckily for the spider, spider-eating birds and lizards can't see it on the flower either.

The second type of camouflage is *countershading.* A countershaded animal is darkest on the top of its body, where the most light strikes it, and lightest on the bottom, where it receives the least light. Most mammals, many birds, and almost all species of fish are light on the underside of their bodies and dark on the top of their bodies. From a distance they seem to turn into one color and look flat.

Animals with striking markings are camouflaged by *disruptive coloration.* The diamondback rattlesnake of the eastern United States stands out clearly when you see it against a plain background. But when it's moving among grasses, rocks, and sticks, the snake seems to disappear completely. That's because the rattler's black-and-yellow

The arctic fox's white winter coat blends
into its snow-covered surroundings, making
it difficult for enemies and prey animals
to spot it. A fox's hearing is so good,
it can hear a mouse running through a
narrow tunnel under five inches
(12.7 cm) of hard-packed snow.

Copperhead snakes are so well camouflaged that they can live near people their entire lives without detection.

Can you tell which part is the leaf and which is the leaf mantis?

pattern leads the eye away from the animal's shape and into the background. For the same reason, a zebra's stripes actually hide the zebra from predators when it grazes near trees and bushes.

OTHER KINDS OF CAMOUFLAGE

Nature has even more camouflage tricks up her sleeve. Animals like the arctic wolf and fox change color with the seasons. They have dark coats in summer, when the ground is dry and brown. But after the snow flies in winter, they sport a snowy white coat that hides them from predators and prey alike.

Some predators, like the octopus, and fish, like groupers, can change color as they move from one background to another to confuse or become invisible to prey.

Mimicry, or imitation, of an animal is another kind of camouflage. There are many small fish called wrasses that clean particles of food from between the teeth of larger fish. A fish called a blenny mimics these cleaners because it has a similar color, shape, size, and way of moving. The blenny uses these features as a disguise to get near enough to a big fish to take bites out of it.

Bright coloration is still another kind of camouflage. It usually warns enemies that "I am dangerous." Some prey animals, like the ladybug beetle, taste especially unpleasant. Others really are dangerous. A bird that takes a bite of a red-and-black arrow poison frog is in for a nasty surprise. If the bird survives, it won't make that mistake again.

5

HUNTING STYLES—GOTCHA!

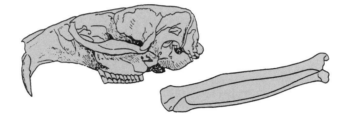

Despite all of their wonderful adaptations for hunting and killing, top predators live a life of either feast or famine. Often, large hunters like lions, tigers, and wolves go hungry for days, even weeks, at a time. Sometimes prey is scarce, and often not-so-helpless prey animals escape by running away or by fighting back with flying legs or sharp antlers.

In fact, big predators come away empty-handed most of the time when attempting a kill. Not every hunt is a dramatic fight-to-the-finish confrontation, either. Some of the largest whales in the ocean, including the biggest predator of all, the over 100-foot-long (30.5 m) blue whale, feed on zooplankton, (marine animals about an inch long (2.5 cm) or smaller). They catch these little animals by filtering sea water through brushes of whalebone called baleen that hang from their jaws.

To add to the food they get by hunting, many predators

also steal food from each other. Bald eagles may snatch fish from on osprey in midair. Lions occasionally raid hyenas' kills. And hyenas steal food from almost any animal on the African plain—jackals, cheetahs, leopards, and even lions. Grizzly bears, vultures, and hyenas also eat carrion, which is the flesh of a dead animal that may have been rotting for days or weeks.

To catch their prey, predators use many different hunting techniques. Some even use a combination of techniques, depending on the season, the terrain on which they live, and the size and speed of their prey.

THE AMBUSH

Predators hunt to feed themselves and their offspring. Some predators *ambush* their meals by waiting patiently out of sight behind a rock or under a leaf until their prey passes by. Then they rush out and grab their surprised victims. A high-speed attack may occur so quickly that a flock of birds may not even notice that one of their number is missing.

Ambushers include web-building spiders that wait for insects to blunder into their nets and ant lions that sit at the bottom of a sand trap until prey falls in.

Some predators use lures like the ones people use to catch fish. The tip of the alligator snapping turtle's tongue looks like a wriggling red worm. When a fish tries to eat the "worm," the turtle's jaws snap shut on the fish.

The copperhead snake coils itself up and lies quietly until a frog or a lizard happens along. Then it waves the tip of its bright yellow tail. Curiosity or hunger makes the prey approach closer until, lightning fast, the snake strikes!

A jackal waits its turn as vultures devour the remains of a carcass killed by another predator.

A bird of prey can ambush a meal from high in the air, or from a tree, a cliff, or any place with a good open view. When a raptor spies a small bird or a rodent, it pulls its wings together and begins a headfirst dive, called a stoop.

The stoop of a diving peregrine falcon has been clocked at over 200 miles (321.8 km) per hour, making it the fastest bird alive. At the instant before striking, the falcon lowers its deadly talons, killing its prey with a blow from its feet.

THE STALK

Many predators stalk, or sneak up on, prey by hiding behind plants, rocks, or trees until they're close enough to pounce. Big cats are expert stalkers. So are alligators, snakes, and polar bears.

A stalking lion tries to make itself smaller by crouching low and keeping its head down. That way, it's less likely to be seen by a gazelle or a wildebeest. The big cat moves closer only when its victim is looking the other way. Should the gazelle look up, the lion freezes in its tracks. When it's near enough, the lion will dash toward its *quarry* at full speed and jump on its back or knock it down with a huge swipe of its paw. Then it will kill by sinking its long canines into the animal's neck.

THE CHASE

When your food can run, fly, or swim away from you, you'd better be pretty fast yourself. And predators who chase

(Above) An African
fishing eagle
ambushes a meal.
(Right) A white
crab spider "hiding"
in full view on a
white flower ambushes
a bronze copper
butterfly.

their prey are fast, though they may lie in wait or stalk prey until they're within chasing range.

The cheetah is the fastest animal on land. With its slim build, long legs, and supple spine, a cheetah can run up to 70 miles (112.6 km) per hour—faster than most birds fly. But like all cats, the cheetah tires quickly. After an all-out chase of about a quarter of a mile (.40 km), the cheetah must rest for at least half an hour before it can run again at full speed.

Wolves, foxes, and coyotes are members of the dog, or canine, family. Dogs have more stamina than cats and can chase their victims for a very long time. A wolf can trot after a rabbit at about 25 miles (40 km) per hour for 25 minutes without stopping to rest. If the rabbit tires before the wolf, the wolf has its meal.

Two or more coyotes may chase prey in relays. As one coyote drives rabbits in circles, the others rest. Once in a while, a rested coyote joins in the chase until the rabbit is tired and can be easily brought down.

Raptors can chase other birds at speeds between 40 to 60 miles (64 to 96.5 km) per hour. When pursuing a smaller bird in flight, a raptor often sweeps beneath it and, turning on its back, thrusts its talons into the prey's breast, killing it instantly.

HUNTING AS A TEAM

If you wanted to move a really big rock, you'd probably ask some friends for help. In the same way, predators who want to make a meal of an animal much larger than themselves hunt as a team.

*The fastest animal predator in the world
is the cheetah, shown here
in hot pursuit of an impala.*

In fact, *social carnivores* like wolves, lions, hyenas, coyotes, and killer whales always live and hunt in family groups. That way, in addition to hunting together, they can protect their offspring from other large predators.

The wolf's family group is called a pack. Wolves hunting alone may capture small animals like beavers, rabbits, hares, mice, and birds. But working together, a pack of wolves can bring down large prey like moose, deer, caribou, elk, and mountain sheep.

Lions are the only big cats that hunt as a team. Working together, these lions have brought down a zebra.

Orcas, or killer whales, live in family groups called pods. When they hunt salmon, pod members stretch out in a straight line and "herd" the fish. As the whale circle closes in around the fish, the whales slap their tails to keep the salmon together. Like wolves, orcas use their superior speed and team strength to pack-hunt whales two to three times larger than themselves.

There's even a tropical insect that hunts as part of a deadly team. Half-inch-long (1.3 cm) South American army ants travel in the tens of thousands and devour every living thing in their path. Insects, snakes, livestock, horses, rats, mice . . . even people and crocodiles are no match for army ants on the march!

6
PREDATORS AND PEOPLE

Throughout history, people have had a love-hate relationship with predators. Because predators kill other animals to survive, they arouse our strong emotions. On the one hand, many cultures respect predators. The ancient Egyptians worshipped wolves and falcons as gods. The Sioux Indians regarded rattlesnakes as their cousins. Some Indian nations consider the owl a wise and friendly spirit.

On the other hand, many cultures have turned predators into villains. Folk tales and fables like the Three Little Pigs make predators like the wolf appear greedy, cunning, and vicious. And many peoples have systematically killed predators. The ancient Greeks paid bounties, or rewards of money, to people who killed wolves. In Shakespeare's time, many European predators including crows, hawks, and weasels had a price on their heads because they competed with people for food—fish, fowl, and game animals.

Even today, top predators who have little to fear from other animals still have much to fear from people. Until recently, the United States government paid bounties to people who killed grizzly bears, mountain lions, and timber wolves. In the 1930s, wolves and cougars were shot or poisoned throughout our national parks. Until the 1950s, states such as Alaska even paid hunters to kill our national symbol, the bald eagle.

These "anti-predator" campaigns succeeded in wiping out entire species of animals. The sea mink, which once lived on the East Coast of North America, is now *extinct.* So are almost all of the subspecies of wolves that used to live in the lower forty-eight United States.

Grizzly bears, mountain lions, and timber wolves are now considered *endangered species,* or animals who are in danger of dying out completely.

COMPETITION FOR SPACE

A decreasing amount of territory is another threat to predators' survival. A territory is the land that a predator needs to hunt, mate, and raise its young. A population of lions may require a territory of hundreds or even thousands of square miles. When a territory becomes full of farms, ranches, highways, and shopping malls, it can't support enough prey animals to feed the predators that live in it. When predators lose their food supply, they either die out or end up eating garbage or killing domestic animals.

The grizzly bear used to be found across the entire western United States, and the North American mountain

*Today mountain lions (also called cougars
or panthers) are found only in the wilder
parts of several western states,
southwest Canada, and Mexico.*

lion once lived all across the continent. Today, grizzly bears live in only a few protected areas, including Wyoming's Yellowstone National Park and Montana's Glacier National Park. Figure 5 gives a demographic profile of the grizzly bear and three other endangered top predators.

Many attacks on people from so-called "man-eating" predators—bears, wolves, and lions—have been the result of this competition for space. When territories shrink, predator—people encounters increase. Nevertheless, most predators almost never harm people unless they are provoked. For example, a mother bear may strike out at a human being to protect her cubs if she believes that a person has come too close for comfort.

OUR CHANGING VIEWS

Fortunately for us and for predators, over the last fifty years, there's been a remarkable change in peoples' attitudes toward predators. We are finally beginning to admire the strength, speed, beauty, and cunning of predators. We are also beginning to understand that they play an essential role in maintaining all forms of life.

Without predators, the world might be overrun with prey animals like insects, mice, and rabbits. Predators actually ensure that prey animals stay strong and healthy. That's because no predator will attack a fit, active animal that's capable of fighting back when it can more easily take an old, sick, injured, or young animal. This means that only the fittest prey animals survive to reproduce.

Today, we are trying to reverse the damage done to

FIGURE 5.
THE STRUGGLE FOR LIFE
ENDANGERED NORTH AMERICAN APEX PREDATORS

SPECIES	PAST RANGE AND POPULATION	CURRENT RANGE AND POPULATION
GRIZZLY BEAR	All of North America west of the Mississippi River from Alaska to Mexico (perhaps 100,000)	Alaska, western Canada, Yellowstone National Park, northern Montana, and Washington State (1 percent of its former range/fewer than 300)
GRAY WOLF	All of North America; twenty-four subspecies	Alaska, western Canada, Minnesota, Montana; six subspecies
BALD EAGLE	Southern bald eagle—all of the United States south of New Jersey and west to California. In 1860, estimated breeding pairs equaled 50,000	In 1960, less than 400 breeding pairs existed, two thirds of these in Florida. Now there are over 2,600 breeding pairs.
PEREGRINE FALCON	North America and Europe. In 1940, 400 breeding pairs in the eastern United States	In 1978, no breeding pairs left in the eastern United States. Reintroduced and brought up to twenty-seven breeding pairs in 1984

A red fox in autumn. Despite the growth of cities, the red fox survives surprisingly well in urban areas.

predators by setting up programs to help save them. Peregrine falcons are now bred in captivity in a number of states and released into wild areas where they once lived. Using birds from Canada and Alaska, bald eagle reintroduction programs in seventeen states have brought this magnificent bird back from the edge of extinction.

In 1989, two pairs of red wolves raised in captivity were released in North Carolina's Alligator River National Wildlife Refuge. Since then, they've given birth to cubs. This marks the first time that people have successfully restored a predator extinct in the wild to its natural habitat.

Most top predators are now protected by international law. In the United States, it is illegal to harm any bird of prey, even if it is not endangered. International laws also protect predators like polar bears and killer whales that roam from country to country. Even countries in which land is scarce are doing their part. In India, protected parks and wildlife refuges have been set aside to allow some species of tigers and panthers to live and breed.

This is not to say that predators don't remain a source of controversy. Many people still believe predators are evil. In the western United States, people continue to kill snakes by the hundreds at rattlesnake roundups. And many farmers and ranchers want to destroy the coyotes, cougars, foxes, bears, and bobcats that kill their livestock.

But as you've just learned, predators are important. So the next time you hear about the "big bad wolf," don't you believe it!

GLOSSARY

Ambush—a trap in which hidden predators lie in wait to attack their prey by surprise.

Apex predators—the largest and strongest predators (also called top predators).

Camouflage—a disguise or behavior that an animal uses to hide itself or deceive an enemy.

Carnivores—flesh-eating animals (also called strict predators).

Color resemblance—a type of camouflage in which an animal's natural color matches its surroundings.

Compound eye—an eye with more than one lens.

Countershading—a type of camouflage in which the top of an animal's body is dark colored and the bottom is light colored.

Disruptive coloration—a boldly patterned coloring that breaks up the shape of an animal and makes it hard to recognize.

Echolocation—a method of locating distant or invisible objects, like prey, by means of sound waves reflected back to the predator.

Endangered species—animals threatened with extinction (see *extinct*).

Extinct—no longer in existence.

Fang (also called a **canine**)—a long, pointed tooth used to grip and hold prey; when hollow, sometimes used to inject poison.

Infrared light—invisible light rays that have a penetrating heating effect.

Lateral-line system—fluid-filled canals beneath the surface of the skin, usually that of a fish.

Mimicry—a type of camouflage in which one animal looks like another animal.

Omnivores—animals that eat meat and plants (also called part-time predators).

Pesticide—a poison used to kill insects.

Photosynthesis—the way in which plants turn the sun's energy into food.

Predators—animals that live by hunting and eating other animals.

Prey—an animal hunted for food by another animal.

Quarry—an animal that is hunted or pursued.

Raptor—a bird of prey.

Social carnivores—meat-eating animals that live and hunt in family groups.

Sonar—a device that detects the location of an underwater object (like a submarine) by means of waves reflected to and from the object.

Stinger—a sharp organ connected to a poison gland that is able to wound by piercing and injecting a poisonous fluid.

Tentacle—a long flexible extension from the body that an animal uses for grasping and feeling.

Ultrasonic—a sound too high-pitched for the human ear to hear.

FURTHER READING

Eaton, Randall L. *The Cheetah: Nature's Fastest Racer.* New York: Dodd, Mead, 1981.

Patent, Dorothy Hinshaw. *Bears of the World.* New York: Holiday House, 1980.

Patent, Dorothy Hinshaw. *The Lives of Spiders.* New York: Holiday House, 1980.

Johnson, Sylvia A., and Aamodt, Alice. *Wolf Pack: Tracking Wolves in the Wild.* Minneapolis: Lerner, 1985.

Lavine, Sigmund A. *Wonders of Coyotes.* New York: Dodd, Mead, 1984.

Ranger Rick Books. *Endangered Animals.* National Wildlife Federation, 1989.

INDEX

ABOUT THE AUTHOR

Predators! is the first children's book for the Salzberg husband-and-wife team. Anita Baskin-Salzberg holds a master's in art and teaching from Northwestern University and works as a free-lance copywriter. Allen Salzberg is a free-lance publicist and writer on the environment. He is also a board member of the New York Turtle and Tortoise Society.

The Salzbergs have sold articles on turtles and horse-shoe crabs to *Ranger Rick.* In addition their articles have appeared in *Omni, Outside* magazine, and *E: The Environmental Magazine.* They are now writing a book about flightless birds for Franklin Watts.

The Salzbergs live in Forest Hills, New York.